The Adventures of
TEAM FANTASTIC

A PRACTICAL GUIDE FOR
TEAM LEADERS AND MEMBERS

The Adventures of
TEAM FANTASTIC

A PRACTICAL GUIDE FOR
TEAM LEADERS AND MEMBERS

Glenn L. Hallam

Center for Creative Leadership
Greensboro, North Carolina

The Center for Creative Leadership is an international, nonprofit educational institution founded in 1970 to foster leadership and effective management for the good of society overall. As a part of this mission, it publishes books and reports that aim to contribute to a general process of inquiry and understanding in which ideas related to leadership are raised, exchanged, and evaluated. The ideas presented in its publications are those of the author.

The Center thanks you for supporting its work through the purchase of this volume. If you have comments, suggestions, or questions about any Center publication, please contact Walter W. Tornow, Vice President, Research and Publication, at the address given below.

Center for Creative Leadership
Post Office Box 26300
Greensboro, North Carolina 27438-6300

CENTER FOR CREATIVE LEADERSHIP

CCL No. 172

Library of Congress Cataloging-in-Publication Data

Hallam, Glenn L.
    The adventures of team fantastic : a practical guide for team leaders and members / Glenn L. Hallam.
        p.   cm.
    ISBN 1-882197-17-8
    1. Work groups. 2. Communication in management. 3. Executive ability. I. Title.
HD66.H35 1996
658.4'02—dc20   95-26741
                                                                                       CIP

Table of Contents

Acknowledgments

Thank you, David Campbell, for the freedom, support, and inspiration to take this adventure.

Thanks also to Martin Wilcox, Marcia Horowitz, Joanne Ferguson, Susan Hyne, Dianne Nilsen, and Bill Drath for their extensive guidance as well as the Center for Creative Leadership for the time and freedom to create.

Preface

Although this book makes use of imaginative stories about teamwork, its purpose and background are quite serious. It draws on over fifty years of research in the areas of social and organizational psychology as well as the experience of practitioners working with a wide range of teams in American industry. Even though teams became the hot topic in the eighties and nineties, psychologists have been studying groups for most of the twentieth century. Concepts such as social facilitation, social loafing, group norms, group goal-setting, groupthink, and the risky shift were invented by psychologists to explain their observations long before corporations discovered that teams could boost productivity and quality. When translated into everyday language these concepts explain how people can work together productively as a team. Thus, one goal in writing this book has been to translate research findings into practical tips that can be applied by team members and leaders.

Many of the recommendations presented in this book are based on my experience working with teams, ranging from shop floor assembly teams to management teams of multibillion dollar companies, as a member of the staff at the Center for Creative Leadership in Colorado Springs. These experiences have allowed me to learn firsthand about the internal dynamics, struggles, and successes of real-life teams in American business today.

In this work, I use an assessment tool called the *Campbell-Hallam Team Development Survey*™, the product of a five-year collaboration with David Campbell. The survey measures how a team is functioning in nineteen areas such as mission clarity, team coordination, team unity, and organizational support. By using this device I have been able to collect a large amount of information about hundreds of teams.

The tool has been used by consultants and human resources professionals to assess thousands of teams across North America. If you have completed this instrument and received your report, you will see that each chapter of this book corresponds to an aspect of your team measured by that survey. For example, if you score low on the scale called *Organizational Support,* you may need to devote special attention to chapter 4, "Building Organizational Support."

Many of the teams I have studied have been effective, as measured by their financial performance, track record in meeting their objectives, measures of quality, and the favorable reviews of their customers. Some have been less successful, having missed their deadlines, angered their customers, and even disappointed stockholders. All of them have wanted to improve, which is why I had the opportunity to work with them.

Team members typically want concrete suggestions for how they can improve. I hear questions such as the following:

"We score low in team coordination. What can we do about it?"

"We have a destructive personality clash between two members. How would you suggest we handle this?"

"We don't act like a team and we're not even sure what we're supposed to be doing as a team. What advice would you have for us?"

Of course there are no simple answers to these questions; humans, working in a group, are much more complex than that. Nevertheless, this book provides tips for addressing common challenges such as building organizational support, managing conflict, building skills, coordinating the team's activities, and measuring team performance.

"Great, but do these ideas apply to my team?" you might ask. The recommendations presented apply to any kind of team, whether it is a management, sales, project, or assembly team. They apply whether you consider yourselves self-managed, self-directed, multifunctional, virtual, or ad hoc. This is because these ideas apply to people working in a group.

You will notice that many of the recommendations are phrased for you, the individual team member, not the team as a whole. On the face of it, this seems ironically individualistic for a book on teams. Yet team improvement starts with the initiative of individual contributors, and you are, after all, reading this book as an individual. Ideally, all members of the team will take these actions and indeed most could be acted on by you and your teammates as a group rather than as individuals.

Some of the recommendations will seem obvious, such as "Learn to use the equipment or tools that are now available." Working as a team is not rocket science, and to paraphrase another well-known book, much of what you need to know about working in a team you probably did learn in kindergarten. Yet even teams of rocket scientists overlook what may seem obvious. Members become so preoccupied with their individual responsibilities that they neglect the care and feeding of the team.

In the final chapter I outline a process for acting on the recommendations given here. Obviously, you cannot, and need not, act on all of them. You will want to select the ones that are most important to your team. Ultimately, if you walk away from this book with at least one good idea that you are committed to following through on, you will be on the road to team improvement.

Introduction

You are undoubtedly reading this book because you are a member of a team—perhaps the leader—and you would like this team to be more effective. I have learned some things that I think can help.

There is a challenge in my telling you these things, though. The most memorable, and therefore most useful, way to give you advice is to relate it to the specifics of your situation. But, of course, I don't know the specifics of your situation.

That is why I am inviting you to become a member of another team, a team that we both can know.

I call it *Team Fantastic.*

I chose this name because this imaginary team is gifted with the superhuman ability to travel instantly across time and place. The team is hired on contract for special assignments that require fantastic feats; sometimes I send it on assignments for training purposes only.

The name *Team Fantastic,* however, does not imply that you will always be a success. Like most teams, this one will have to learn from experience. Perhaps it is most appropriate to describe you and your imaginary teammates as fantastic learners on a fantastic journey.

With this said, let's begin.

Chapter 1

Managing the Time Crunch

It's the year 2124. NASA is exploring the feasibility of sending people to live on the moon, in preparation for building a space station there. The space agency must determine how people will work, when given a limited oxygen supply. Therefore Team Fantastic has been hired to go to the moon and perform a number of common business tasks. The team will receive whatever equipment or supplies are necessary and scientists will be watching to see what happens.

You and your teammates are strapped to the seats of a rocket, counting down, "ten, nine, eight, seven . . ."

After landing on the moon, the team receives its final order: Stay until you have accomplished your team goals or until your fuel and oxygen supplies are depleted, whichever comes first.

If you were a team of astronauts, you would work efficiently to accomplish the vast array of experiments that have been planned. But you are not astronauts, and that's not how you use your time. You hold lengthy, unproductive meetings. Tick, tick, down go your fuel gauges. You spend hours on the phone. Tick, tick, down go your oxygen gauges. You fumble around with ill-conceived plans before finally getting on track. Tick, tick, tick. At this rate, your fuel gauges will soon read empty and you will find yourselves gasping for air.

There is nothing like the threat of oxygen deprivation to put a team in high gear. Short of cutting off the oxygen, however, your real-life team can take several steps to make better use of time back on Earth. By taking these actions, you and your team can benefit from the advantages of teamwork without falling prey to one of the greatest disadvantages: wasted time.

Ways to Help

Prioritize team projects or responsibilities. One way to do this is to list your team's five largest projects and ask members to rank their importance. Then, calculate the average ranks. A less formal approach is to say to teammates, "I know you are running around like chickens with their heads cut off. Is there anything we're doing that doesn't really have to be done now?" If your teammates speak their minds, they may help you develop a strategy for focusing the team's attention on what really counts.

Drive productive meetings with pointed questions. At the start of meetings, ask questions such as the following:

- What do we absolutely have to accomplish today?
- What decisions need to be made?
- How long do we plan to meet?
- Do we all need to be here for this discussion?

If a meeting begins to drag on, ask these kinds of questions:

- How can we get some closure on this?
- What do you need from me?
- What are we going to do and who is going to do it?
- Do we have enough information at this time to make a decision, or should we move on to the next topic?

Count your minutes. If you wanted to lose weight, you'd probably start by counting calories. Similarly, if you want to reduce the time you waste, start by counting minutes. How long do you spend in meetings? At the water cooler or coffee pot? On the phone? Only by recording how you spend your time can you find ways to spend it more wisely. Try this for a day. You might be surprised by what you find.

Be honest with callers about how much time you have to talk. Many of us rival social teenagers in the time we spend on the phone. To avoid long conversations, try greeting the caller as follows: "Hello, Pat, good to hear from you. Listen, I've got just a few minutes to talk now; is that all right?"

Setting expectations in this manner will result in shorter, more productive conversations, especially when Pat loves to talk.

Study the accuracy of your planning predictions. We all try to plan realistically, yet we sometimes find ourselves in a panic, having underestimated the complexity of the job. After completing a task, determine whether you over- or underestimated how long it would take to do it. For example, examine old memos or timetables to see how long you thought the job would take. If you find that you consistently underestimate how long it takes to do a task, you have a common problem that can generate stress and eventually erode your credibility with people who rely on you. Although it is an exaggeration, Murphy's Law may hold a grain of truth for you. In estimating the time to complete a job, make a guess (for example, two hours), multiply this number by two (four hours), and take the next larger unit of measure (four days). That's how long it will take, according to Murphy!

Avoid overcommitting yourself. We often try to please others by saying "yes" to every request that comes our way. "Yes, I'll write that report by tomorrow." "Yes, I'll perform this maintenance task this afternoon." Although a "will do" attitude is essential for succeeding in most organizations, you can sometimes do yourself and others a favor by saying, "I would like to help you, but I don't have time to do it now. How about next week?" It is better to be realistic than to make promises you cannot fulfill (and suffer the stress or guilt that results when you fall behind).

Prioritize the items on your to-do list. Although it is regarded as compulsive behavior by some people, writing to-do lists is a great way to get the load off your mind and onto paper. Many, perhaps most, people do this, but then they neglect to prioritize the tasks. Once you have listed the jobs to be done, rank them by level of urgency or importance, and try to accomplish them in that order.

If the team simply cannot accomplish the work in the allotted time, write a job description for selecting someone who could help. What roles and responsibilities would this person have? What skills, knowledge, or other qualities should this person possess? Whether or not your team has the funds to hire such a person, this exercise may help you understand your team's weak points.

Establish quality control procedures to catch mistakes that are likely to happen when your team is in a hurry. When teams are not wasting time, they often are working under extreme time pressure, which can lead to mistakes. Make certain that at least two people on your team take a final look at your product, whether it be a radio or a report, before it goes out the door. Develop simple standardized checklists for performing complex tasks under time pressure.

Take steps to develop a more coordinated, efficient team. See chapter 8—"Coordinating the Team"—for suggestions in this area.

Chapter 2

Handling the Information Load

Thanks to the threat of oxygen deprivation, Team Fantastic has learned to use its time wisely. It prioritizes its work on the moon and sets about doing the most important tasks first. Meetings begin to run more efficiently and everyone learns to spend less time on the phone. So far the team is learning from its experience and winning the race against oxygen and fuel gauges.

You have found, however, that there is another challenge: handling the information coming your way. On the moon the team has a lot to talk about and much to learn. It needs to know how to operate special equipment, what dangerous areas to avoid, and the location of each member. If a teammate accidentally cuts an oxygen cord, you need to know this right away, before it's too late.

Each of you has a radio that allows you to communicate with each other and Mission Control. Unfortunately, some members don't know how to use their radios, some don't know what questions to ask, and some people simply hoard the information they receive from NASA, neglecting to pass it along. Some people even turn their radios off when they get busy.

When it comes to getting information from Mission Control, it's either feast or famine. The team can go for hours without hearing a word from them; then, all of a sudden, each of you receives a flood of technical information. Of course you don't need to know all of this information, and some of it is unintelligible, but you do your best to absorb what you can.

In this situation, as in the real work world, the team is struggling to manage the information load. There are several steps you can take to meet this challenge.

Ways to Help

Define the information needs of your team. For example, when starting a new project or reviewing your progress, ask your team, "What do we need to know and who do we think can answer our questions?" Urge team members to be as specific as possible in formulating questions that need to be answered.

Divide information-gathering responsibilities among the members to minimize duplication of effort. Have only one trusted person make the call, read the report, or talk to the customer. That one person can summarize the obtained information and pass it along to the other members.

Ask each member to share important news in team meetings. This activity will establish the expectation that members bring and share information. It also will keep members from feeling left out or undervalued, and allow shy members to make a greater contribution.

After each meeting, make sure that minutes are distributed to all members, especially those who were unable to attend. Many teams overlook this obvious step, perhaps because taking notes is perceived as onerous. When minutes are distributed, include a note encouraging members to review what was discussed in the last meeting. For example, you might write, "Here are the minutes from our productive team meeting this week. Please take a moment to review them."

Take advantage of computer technology such as E-mail to streamline the information-gathering and dissemination process. Learn to use the systems available, including advanced features such as message distribution (for sending a message to a group of people). Ensure that members of the team are trained and comfortable with this technology. Try to avoid cluttering the system with messages that have limited value, so reading E-mail does not become viewed as a waste of time.

Develop routine reports, such as weekly team schedules, for distributing repetitive, ongoing information. Once these reports have been developed, the responsibility for continuing them can be delegated to another team member, if desired.

Experiment with simple "sign in, sign out" or other tracking mechanisms. Such a system can be particularly helpful when members travel frequently or work in different locations. Some less formal organizations have the simple rule, "If you leave, just tell Julie where you are going and when you'll be back."

Identify and get to know specific individuals from whom you need important information. Remind these people what you need to know, when you need to know it, and why the information is important to you. Be sure to thank them whenever they provide you with the information you need.

Post important data that are frequently used, such as schedules, production figures, or room assignments. Airline flight arrival and departure monitors are good models. Thousands of people have instant access to important data.

Use simple, eye-catching methods for presenting information to your teammates. Everyone has glossed over a memo because it looked boring or irrelevant. To be certain people read your memos, distill the message down to a series of bullet points, use large, easy-to-read type, and choose a conceptual angle you think will make the information seem interesting and relevant to your readers.

Chapter 3

Exploring Team Tools

Team Fantastic has returned to Earth, having had a successful trip to the moon. Now you are asked to climb aboard a time machine, which takes you to the mid-1800s, when railroads were being built to link the East and West of the United States. Your mission: Lay and straighten five miles of rails.

Surrounded by the massive expanse of the plains, you and your teammates quickly devise a method for the task. After the rails are laid on the ties, the members, each wielding a long crowbar, work in unison. The leader calls out, "one, two, three," and together you nudge the rail straight. Then you move to the next section.

For days, the team creeps along, straightening about a half-mile of track a day. Although it is back-breaking work, your group is the perfect example of coordinated team effort. You are all proud of the few miles of progress you have made.

Then one day the tracks approach an intersection with another set of tracks under construction. In the distance you can see that a team is working on the rails, but this team has fewer members and one member is driving a large contraption that looks like a train. Upon further investigation, you find that this machine straightens the rails as it goes. The other team members are able to concentrate on laying the rails before the machine, then inspecting the track after it has been straightened. They tell you that they are able to lay, straighten, and inspect five miles of rails in one day! No longer does your team feel so proud of its progress.

Industrial history is rife with examples of new machinery revolutionizing how work is done. The revolution continues every day as helpful tools are introduced at a blinding speed. Perhaps there is no tool that could help you as much as the rail-straightening machine helped the railroads, and you probably wouldn't want a machine that just might put you out of a job, but there are probably other tools or equipment that money could buy that would help your team be a little more productive.

Ways to Help

Explore new technologies. Scout out the latest technologies that other teams doing similar work are utilizing. Bring along a creative teammate who can help you determine whether and how the technology can help. Trade conferences are often good places to do this. Collect articles, product reviews, or advertisements from trade journals.

Write a "wish list." For example, ask your team, "If we could buy one tool to make us more productive or creative, what would that be?" Assess the potential payoff of each item. Ask, "How much faster could the work get done? What kinds of innovations would be possible with the new tools? Whose time would be better utilized by having such a resource?"

Prioritize the group's material needs. Ask the team, "Of the tools we have listed which ones seem the most useful to us?"

Explore clever ways to obtain resources. For example, arrange to share resources with another team or to barter work for access to equipment or space. Investigate other budgets that are available in the organization to cover the proposed expenses. Look for less expensive ways to obtain the needed resources, such as leasing, borrowing, or buying used equipment in good condition.

Develop a written justification for obtaining key resources and present this case to the people with the purse strings. Arrange to meet with your boss or the financial people to discuss new possibilities, and leave them with the written case to remind them of your needs.

Learn to use the equipment or tools that are now available. Talk to your teammates about how they use these tools or why they find them useful. Ask them to teach you how to use these tools, or enroll yourself in a training course.

See the ways to obtain organizational support, below. Having strong, positive ties to the rest of the organization can be a great help when new resources are needed.

Chapter 4

Building Organizational Support

After a brief journey forward in time, the time machine lands Team Fantastic in the early 1900s at the edge of a jungle in Brazil. Your mission: Venture into the jungle—overridden by giant snakes, insects the size of birds, a tribe of headhunters, and quicksand—and find a buried chest of priceless diamonds.

Before entering the jungle, you need a few things. You need the right equipment, clothing, and food. You need to learn the appropriate etiquette for interacting with snakes. You need to know which plants are edible and which ones are poisonous as well as the location of the quicksand, headhunters, and diamonds.

You have your orders; it's time to go, and there's no one there to help you. So you venture forth without guns or knowledge of the perils that await you. The only mystery is whether you will end up at the bottom of a pool of quicksand, in the belly of a fat and happy snake, or over a doorway bringing good luck to a headhunter's family.

People assigned to work in teams can be hapless adventurers wandering into a jungle uninformed and undersupplied. Often they are given a task without adequate time, money, talent, and information. The leader is told to go out and lead the team but is not given the opportunity to learn how to be an effective team facilitator or coach. Antiquated reward structures and performance appraisal systems often encourage individual performance rather than teamwork. Is it any surprise that these brave adventurers sometimes end up drowning in quicksand?

Ways to Help

Articulate the needs of your team. Yelling "help" at the edge of a jungle is likely to be less effective than asking your organization for specific kinds of help (for example, "We need guns, medicine, and more information about the perils that await us"). Survey your team's needs so you will know what kinds of help to request. For example, are members getting the information they need to do the job well? (See chapter 2—"Handling the Information Load.") Do the performance appraisal or reward systems need to be modified so that there is a greater incentive to work together as a team? (See chapter 15—"Rewarding Performance.") Does the team need further clarification of its mission? (See chapter 7—"Clarifying the Mission.")

Get to know leaders in your organization who can provide what your team needs. For example, ask them to lunch. Learn more about their interests, hobbies, and families. The result could be that you develop new friends and helpful supporters for your team.

Help others in the organization understand why it is important for them to support you. Talk to key leaders about your team and its mission. Explain to them what you are trying to accomplish and why you need their support. If necessary, redefine your mission so that it corresponds more closely to that of the rest of the organization.

Document and publicize your team's successes. For example, write a memo to key leaders in which you congratulate your teammates on their accomplishments, perhaps in the form of an "update." This will also serve to make your teammates feel more valued.

Ask for nonfinancial support such as training opportunities and feedback on the team's performance. When you go into a jungle, money can't buy a safe and successful journey. You also need information and skills.

Show appreciation for the support you receive. That new computer system may seem overdue and will complicate your life as your team learns to use it, but it is still support. The opportunity to attend a training course may seem like an order from human resources that takes you from your real work, but it is support. Decide whom to thank and show your appreciation to that person (as opposed to complaining when support seems lacking). Small and genuine gestures, such as sending a thank-you note or a T-shirt that has been signed by each member of your team, can go a long way in ensuring that you continue to receive support in the future.

Chapter 5

Building and Utilizing Skills

During the first days in the jungle, Team Fantastic had its ups and downs. Once you all fell into a pit built by headhunters to catch their prey but managed to climb out before they arrived for dinner. If you had a diamond for every time you thought you were about to die you'd be rich by now, but you haven't found any diamonds. Still, miraculously, you are all alive and healthy.

One reason you have survived is because the team took an inventory of members' skills and discovered how each person could best help the team. One of you has sensitive hearing, so this person is now in charge of listening for hissing snakes, beating drums, or other signs of danger. Another person, a former minor league baseball player, wields a mean machete and is responsible for walking in front of the team cutting a path through the jungle. One member revealed that when she was a Girl Scout she learned to use a map and compass, so she's in charge of navigation.

On the verge of disaster, team members were forced to take a hard look at each other's hidden skills and find ways to better utilize them. The stakes are lower in the real work world, but you still might benefit from a careful and deliberate examination of members' skills.

Ways to Help

Identify the critical skills and knowledge that spell the difference between average and superior team performance. What technical skills or intellectual abilities are needed? Does the job require people who are good with numbers? Talented writers? Skilled craftspersons? Clever problem-solvers? Creative dreamers?

What interpersonal skills are needed? Do you need people who can sell the Brooklyn Bridge? Deliver well-organized, entertaining presentations at the drop of a hat? Resolve conflicts between enemies?

Write a brief description of these skills or abilities and note why each is important to effective team performance. For each, indicate whether it needs to be possessed by all, some, or just one of your team members. In the future, you can use this list as a map to help guide hiring and training decisions.

Learn more about your teammates' skills and experience. Watch them on the job and study what they produce. What do they do well? What makes each person unique from the others? Ask each member to talk about his or her key job experiences over the last ten years. Often you will find that you have been unaware of some special skill or knowledge that a team member has to offer.

For each of the skills or areas of knowledge that you think is important to success, indicate who on your team possesses it. For example, who can manipulate numbers? Who writes well? Who is clever at conceptualizing a problem? Who is a good organizer? Who is skilled at noticing details that others overlook? Who is fluent and scintillating in making presentations? Who is good at motivating your team? Who has a gift for handling conflict?

Now ask yourself, "Where are the gaps? What skills or knowledge are either missing or spread too thinly or unevenly among the team members?" Even if you have already gone through this process informally, doing it more formally and deliberately can be revealing.

Seek out the knowledge and opinions of your teammates, especially those who tend not to speak up. Some people can be intimidated by the more dominant members of the group; others are just plain shy. Yet silent members can have terrific ideas.

Develop one new skill or area of knowledge. Pursue development opportunities such as training and special assignments that will make you more useful to your team.

Write a job description for a person who might fill your team's current void in skill or knowledge. What kinds of experience, skills, knowledge, and other characteristics would make this imaginary person the ideal addition to your team? If you can hire such a person, great. Otherwise, this imaginary person can be useful as a symbol for the areas in which your team needs to develop.

Give other team members guidance or tactful feedback when appropriate. Promote honest feedback as a regular part of the team's work. (See chapter 14—"Giving and Receiving Feedback.")

Chapter 6

Building Commitment

Fortunately, you have not been completely abandoned in the jungle. As the drums beat louder and draw closer, you hear a helicopter flying overhead and see a small package crashing through the trees to the ground. The package contains instructions to walk north to the river, where the team will find a raft. The message warns, "Paddle quickly to avoid hidden dangers."

Team Fantastic is now seated together in the raft, paddling down the river. Although most of you are paddling furiously, two members in the back of the boat have fallen asleep. Without full power, the raft has slowed, becoming vulnerable to hidden dangers: alligators that have entered the water and are now converging on the boat. "Wake up! Wake up! Let's get moving!"

Why would these two members fall asleep while others work so hard? Perhaps they are unaware of the alligators. Perhaps they don't care about finding the diamonds. Perhaps they are simply too tired and undernourished to continue paddling. Perhaps they are too comfortable as they drift on a beautiful river in the sun. Perhaps they are in poor physical condition and therefore not capable of helping the team at this moment. Perhaps they are sick. Or perhaps they are trying to send the team a message.

On your real-life team, as on Team Fantastic, a number of factors have to go right for members to be committed. Members need to be psychologically and physically well-nourished, interested in the goals of your team, and aware of the consequences of failure. They need to be capable of expending time and energy for the betterment of your team and not distracted by issues such as personal problems or team conflict.

Member commitment also depends on (and is reflected by) your team's norms: unwritten but powerful rules of acceptable behavior. On your real team are members expected—either implicitly or explicitly—to work late to meet deadlines? Help each other in stressful times? Come to meetings on time? Are they expected to put team interests before their own?

Norms develop soon after a team is formed and are quickly conveyed to new members. Changing them can be difficult, which is why it is important that productive norms be established early in a team's formation. In the beginning of the river journey, if someone on Team Fantastic had said, "Whatever we do, let's not stop paddling—there are hidden dangers out there," the two slumbering passengers may have remained alert.

Ways the Leader or Prominent Member Can Help

Write down what you believe to be the unwritten rules that guide the actions of your team. Here are some examples:

"We do whatever it takes to be the best."

"Members wait for the leader to take initiative, then follow."

"When the pressure is on, everyone gives 110%."

"We work hard enough to meet the minimum requirements, no harder."

Identify which rules seem beneficial and which ones are obstacles.

Explicitly set new team norms. Discuss as a team how you want to behave together. (This exercise will apply to many aspects of teamwork, not just commitment.) Embrace the positive norms of the past. Set new norms to replace unhelpful ones.

Live the new team norms. Make it obvious that you are honoring your commitment to these norms. Your example—whether it reflects deep concern for the team or complete apathy—will be noticed by your teammates.

Assign well-defined tasks to specific individuals and hold them accountable. This will help to counteract a phenomenon called *social loafing:* In large teams members sometimes slow down, knowing that they can rely on star performers to carry the team to success. If the members of Team Fantastic who stopped paddling were in their own rafts and solely responsible for their fate, they might have paddled their hearts out.

Grant members more control over their work. If you have confidence in them, allow members to take personal initiative and exercise discretion. (See chapter 11—"Empowering Yourself and Teammates.")

Give members the opportunity to perform a number of different activities to broaden their skills and perspectives. Members will come to enjoy work that is varied and challenging.

Allow members to produce a whole and visible piece of work. Members are more likely to enjoy their work and become personally invested in it if they can look at the outcome of their work and say, "We did that."

Introduce members to their constituents. Members tend to be more committed when they realize the significance of their work—for the organization, customer, or society as a whole. Such an appreciation can be gained by meeting and talking to the people who rely on the work of the team.

Minimize outside distractions. To use an example from athletics, if a star quarterback is failing classes, a competent coach will arrange for tutoring. Similarly, a good coach in the business setting will attend to the personal problems and distractions experienced by the members. For instance, encourage your teammates to utilize your company's employee-assistance program to address personal problems and work with your teammates to avoid scheduling conflicts.

Keep your team small. In small groups (no more than fifteen and preferably fewer than ten), members generally receive more rewards and feedback, have more influence within the group, and are more accountable. The result is that members sometimes feel more committed to smaller teams.

Gather members together so they work in physical proximity, or at least provide ample opportunity for members to interact. Members can be energized by the encouragement (and pressure) they receive from each other. (This phenomenon is known as *social facilitation.*)

Ways All Members Can Help

Set a positive example of commitment. If you want to change the team, start with yourself. If you set a clear, conspicuous, and consistent example of commitment, other members will notice; some may follow.

See other topics in this book that relate to commitment. For example, set clear personal goals. (See chapter 10—"Clarifying Personal Goals.") As a team, clarify and reinforce your mission. (See chapter 7—"Clarifying the Mission.") Explore whether members are properly rewarded for their work. (See chapter 15—"Rewarding Performance.")

Chapter 7

Clarifying the Mission

Team Fantastic finally located the diamonds and, with the exception of a few bug bites, has emerged from the jungle healthy and proud. So far, the team has successfully accomplished all missions: You survived the moon, straightened five miles of railroad track, and found the diamonds.

One reason you have succeeded is that the goals of these missions have been clear. A well-defined mission—one that includes goals—acts as a funnel, gathering energy, skill, and knowledge and concentrating these resources for maximum effect.

General goals such as satisfying customers and achieving financial success are helpful but not nearly as motivating as more specific ones, such as 100% customer satisfaction as measured by an end-of-year customer survey; completion of the advanced widget device by June of this year; less than .01% defects, as determined by quality control; 25% growth in profits over the next two years; and 0% turnover for reasons of dissatisfaction with your team.

Specific goals such as these give the mission meat and meaning. They cause members to develop strategies and mobilize resources. In short, they help the team turn the mission into action.

Ways to Help

Discuss the team's reason for being. What purposes does the team serve? Which purpose is most important? Who are your customers, clients, or constituents? What person or group is most important to keep happy in the long run? In the short run? What constitutes quality? If your customers were to rate your team's product or service, what would be the dimensions of quality?

Write a brief statement of team purpose. Incorporate your answers to the above questions about your reason for being.

Set specific, achievable goals for the year. Write them down and ensure that all members both understand and accept them. Focus on a small number of crucial goals rather than an overwhelming array.

Share your purpose or goals with important people outside the team. Making the purpose and goals public can increase the team's commitment to them. Some teams even have their mission printed on business cards.

    Post a statement of your purpose and goals in your work area. Change the location periodically, so members are more likely to notice and read it.

    Seek clarification of how your current tasks fit the team mission. If your own work seems to have little relevance to the purpose or goals of the team, address this issue with your teammates.

    Measure progress toward team goals. Explore ways to measure and plot progress in achieving team goals. A visual plot of progress (such as a graph of the number of goals attained compared to the number outstanding), if updated periodically, can provide powerful feedback and keep the goals alive.

QUALITY IS EVER FASTER, EVER CHEAPER, EVER MORE RELIABLE, EVER MORE INNOVATIVE, AND EVER SIMPLER!

THAT RULES OUT MY AUTOMOBILE.

MY COOKING FAILS THAT STANDARD.

Chapter 8

Coordinating the Team

For its next adventure, Team Fantastic is transported to a park in the Midwest in the 1920s. The mission is a team test: Ride a bicycle around Swimmer's Lake. Make it all the way around before dark and without anyone getting hurt.

You find a bicycle shop on the shore of the lake, where you learn that this will be more than a relaxing ride in the park. When you were told to ride "a bicycle" around the lake, this meant *one* bike for the entire team. Waiting for you is a bicycle that has been specially built so that each member has his or her own seat and pedals, and the person in the front is the only one who can steer, shift the gears, or apply the brakes.

Having learned to tap hidden skills in the jungle, the team is sensitive to this issue, so someone asks, "Anyone here good at riding a bike?" As it turns out, one member is an expert cyclist who races on the weekend, so this person is chosen to ride in front as your leader.

Everyone climbs onto the bicycle and gets ready to pedal. It lurches forward as you try to get on, but then stops, as two people have already fallen off. They get back on, the bike lurches forward again, then stops again. You're off to a rough start.

After a few false starts, you all finally manage to get onto the bike and are pedaling steadily around the lake, the leader skillfully steering, braking, and shifting.

Everything is going fine until a family of ducks waddles across the path and blocks the way. No one says anything about the ducks, though. The people on the back don't even know the ducks are there. Suddenly, the bike stops. Half the members lean to the left, half to the right. The bike teeters left, then right, then falls to the ground. As you lie on your back looking up at the trees, you can hear the ducks quacking as if laughing hysterically at the spectacle of the crash.

Clear, open, conflict-free communication is essential in all teams. To avoid this embarrassing result, the leader needs to communicate clearly with the other members, especially when starting and stopping: "Okay, we're slowing down . . . coming to a stop . . . right foot down." When starting up again, the leader needs to say, "Okay, let's prepare to start . . . left foot on the ground . . . right pedal up . . . ready, set, go."

Unfortunately, leaders who may have excelled as individual performers can become so preoccupied with their own jobs and concerns that they forget to communicate. As you mount the bike and start riding again you realize your leader, who is an accomplished cyclist, is concentrating just on steering, shifting, and braking, and seems either unable or unwilling to communicate at crucial times. You hope for the best and plead with the ducks, "Please, stay off the path!"

A group's norms can spell the difference between coordination and chaos. Your real-life team may have the unwritten rule that it is okay to work independently without informing teammates about your actions and plans. The price for this freedom can be wasted time, effort, and skill. Two people end up doing the same piece of work, or one person spends hours trying to solve a problem that could be solved in minutes by another person with unique skill or experience.

Ways to Help

Start tasks by discussing goals and strategy. Teams sometimes leap into work without thinking strategically about how to approach it. They waste hours following the wrong strategy, then backtrack to another approach. Start tasks by saying, "Before we get into this project, let's talk about how we should approach it. What is our goal and how are we going to achieve it?" If, before getting on the bike, the leader had called a brief meeting to discuss starting and stopping the bike, Team Fantastic might have avoided bruises and embarrassment.

Assign work to individuals. As you undoubtedly know from experience, not all work should be done by the group. Difficult tasks that require great concentration are often best assigned to individual members, who can then report their work back to the team for constructive feedback and further development. The result can be high-quality work that has benefited from team input but not required extensive team coordination.

Organize short "stand-up" meetings to discuss the day or week ahead. Ask each member to summarize what is on that person's agenda for the week and what support he or she will need from the other members. If more discussion of certain topics seems necessary, set aside a time to meet later in the week.

Choose a time and place to conduct long-range planning. This may be at an annual retreat. Be certain that your team has collected information needed to aid in the development of these plans. Arrange to follow up on your plans at a predetermined time.

Set an example by planning ahead and keeping teammates informed about your activities. Tell your teammates what you have coming up and what support you might need. For example, "I have a big deadline this Friday, so I will need the copy machine and extra support on Thursday afternoon" or, "I'll need the sales projections by noon tomorrow so I can send our report out by the end of the week" or, "I've been asked to help in another department on Thursday, so I won't be available that day."

Write an informal definition of your job and share it with other members. Encourage others to do the same. In many teams there is considerable confusion about who is supposed to do what. You may find your teammates define your job differently than you do. (See chapter 10— "Clarifying Personal Goals"— for further suggestions in this area.)

Take steps to better handle your team's information load. See chapter 2—"Handling the Information Load"—for further suggestions.

Chapter 9

Managing Conflict

In spite of the letdowns and failures experienced so far, members of Team Fantastic have gotten along pretty well. You were angry when your teammates fell asleep in the raft but handled this problem in an open, healthy way once you eluded the alligators. The team was bruised, exhausted, and disappointed with the leader by the time you returned to the bicycle shop, but after talking openly about this fiasco you realized what the team had done wrong and vowed to make changes next time.

In both these events, Team Fantastic turned potentially damaging conflict into a helpful lesson that could benefit the team in the future. Members focused on getting the job done and learning from the experience. If members focus on the work and take responsibility for their problems, they have neither the time, energy, nor interest to fight with each other.

Also, going on these exciting journeys together has given members the opportunity to get to know each other and develop trust. Through the rain in the jungle, you all stayed together. When the sun beat down on your backs as you straightened rails, your teammates were there to encourage you and keep you company. Most importantly, you have experienced success together. Shared success breeds positive feelings and attraction between members; when people like each other they obviously are less likely to hurt each other, bicker or fight.

On the other hand, failure often creates conflict, especially when members respond by blaming each other rather than accepting responsibility. Had you reacted to the biking fiasco by blaming the leader, this could have created friction between team members, and the team would never have learned from the situation.

Although conflict is not necessarily destructive, it can be paralyzing. Teams waste time, energy, skills, and money on resolving (or avoiding) it. In the grip of conflict, members cease to share information or help each other in any way. Furthermore, conflict can precipitate a dangerous cycle: People who feel hurt by or angry with each other often stop talking openly. They don't explain themselves and as a result they misinterpret each other's actions, assuming the worst, and then they constantly gather new information to bolster their negative feelings. These feelings in turn prevent them from talking openly with each other, and the insidious cycle continues: (1) feel hurt or angry, (2) fail to communicate, (3) need to assume other's intentions,

(4) assume the worst. Breaking this cycle requires opening communication between the disputing people so they no longer need to assume each other's intentions and can understand why each other thinks, feels, and acts the way they do. As you probably know from experience, this is easier said than done.

At the other extreme, if there is never any conflict among members, or if conflict is avoided at all costs, the team runs the risk of falling into "groupthink"—the inability to critically evaluate itself and its work. As the crew of a ship, members can become so busy patting each other on the back that they run the vessel aground. Teammates who get along well also can waste time chatting or joking excessively when there is work to be done. If this is the case, they need to formulate norms that reflect a better balance of work and play.

In summary, teams have the challenge of minimizing destructive conflict while encouraging constructive disagreement and open debate.

Ways to Minimize Destructive Conflict

Encourage members to switch perspectives. Ask two members who disagree to express their opinions on the controversial issue at hand, then have them switch roles and argue from the other person's perspective. Each will begin to see that the other's perspective is not sinister at all but actually quite reasonable given the circumstances.

Encourage open communication about each member's priorities. When resolving a controversy, it is often helpful to articulate the factors to be considered and to have each member prioritize these factors. For example, one member might say, "In making this decision, I see minimizing downtime as number one, using our existing technology as number two, integrating our system with that of the other departments as number three," and so on.

Some teams create a matrix that lists factors to be considered across the top, names of members down the left, and priority ratings in the cells. Once each member has made his or her priority ratings, the average priorities can be calculated for each factor, and the group has a blueprint for resolving the conflict. The leader might then say, "On average, using existing technology came in first and minimizing downtime came in second. If we follow these priorities, what decision would we make?"

Propose a modification of your team's performance appraisal system so that people are evaluated on how they handle conflict. For example, add a dimension called "handling conflict constructively" to your evaluation forms.

When possible, select new, upbeat team members who will have a positive impact on your team. One playful optimist can change the climate of an entire team. Look for people who have demonstrated an ability to be pleasant and happy in other team settings.

Participate in a team-development program. Studies of their effect often report improved cohesion and communication. Call your human resources director to get the names and numbers of recommended consultants and organizations that provide this service.

Make "good news" an agenda item for team meetings. To raise the team's spirits, celebrate successes, including modest weekly or monthly "wins." Occasionally start your team meetings by saying, "Okay, before we dive into our other business, let's celebrate the positive. What is going well?" Making this a habit can be especially important (and difficult) if you and your teammates are highly goal-oriented and critical.

Say "hello" to teammates and find out how they are doing. This can help lay the groundwork for resolving conflicts when they arise. When you need a break, go visit your co-workers. If you have gained a reputation as task-oriented and unsocial, your co-workers may wonder what is up your sleeve; but in time, as you make a habit of socializing, both you and your teammates will learn to enjoy each other more.

Get to know teammates in a relaxed atmosphere. For example, go out to lunch or take a jog with one of your teammates. By spending quality time with them away from work, you can develop relationships that will weather conflict and competition.

Offer to help your teammates. Your teammates are likely to respond in kind. (This phenomenon is known as the "norm of reciprocity.") A single halfhearted offer of help, however, will probably not produce any results. Over time, by helping your teammates you will develop trust and goodwill that will help you and your teammates weather conflict.

Care for your mental and physical health so you are able to be a positive influence on your team. If personal problems are bothering you, find someone to talk to about the problems, take time to write down your thoughts and feelings, or seek help from a qualified mental health professional. A team is only as healthy as its members.

"Walk a mile in another's shoes" before finding fault or assigning blame. Many conflicts start or grow because of misunderstanding. Rather than letting yourself boil over as you devise evil explanations for the behavior of those around you, ask them why they did what they did. The reasons are usually less sinister than you imagine them to be.

Explain your actions before others invent their own explanations. If your teammates mistrust you, help them understand you.

Focus on solutions without blaming others. Treat conflict as a challenging problem like other work problems you or your team handle. Define the problem, develop reasonable solutions, and implement them.

Avoid forming cliques to complain about problems that should be discussed openly. Forming factions within your team is unhealthy. Resist gossiping, especially when it means criticizing others without giving them an opportunity to reply. If the only way to get it off your chest is to complain, turn to a friend or relative who is willing to listen. Complaining to one teammate about another fans the flames of conflict.

Ways to Promote Healthy Conflict

Have a member play the role of devil's advocate. For example, say to your team, "Since this is an important decision we have to make, let's have someone try to poke holes in our logic."

Divide your team into subgroups to reach independent decisions about a common question, then bring them back together to resolve differences. Divergent opinions are more likely to be expressed when members are in smaller subgroups.

Invite outside experts with different opinions. Have them share their views with your team in an atmosphere of open debate.

Plan, on occasion, to have your team openly evaluate its strengths and weaknesses (see chapter 12—"Reviewing the Past"). Encourage open feedback (see chapter 14—"Giving and Receiving Feedback") and empower team members to speak their minds (see chapter 11—"Empowering Yourself and Teammates").

Chapter 10

Clarifying Personal Goals

When riding the bike, each member of Team Fantastic had the same goal—getting around the lake—and all of you except the leader had the same responsibilities—pedaling hard and staying balanced. Some teams in the real world are like this: Everyone shares a team goal and each person has the same role and responsibilities.

Most work, however, requires the team to organize itself the way Team Fantastic did in the jungle: Each member had a different role and responsibilities. One person listened for predators and another person navigated, for example. The payoff for organizing the team this way is that each member can put special skills to use for the benefit of the team.

Unfortunately, members can become confused about their roles, either because no one knows what these roles are or because the roles have not been clearly articulated. This is common when roles change, as they often do. For example, the Team Fantastic navigator was selected based on her ability to read a map and compass, but over time she took on the responsibility of assessing the risks of alternative routes and guiding the team away from quicksand and headhunters. Roles should evolve like this to fit the abilities of the team member, to meet the needs of the task, or both.

Each member needs to clarify his or her role as responsibilities shift. "I'm looking out for predators coming up from behind," says one member of Team Fantastic. "I'm doing the navigation, as usual, but now I'm also helping to strategize so we don't walk into dangerous situations," says the navigator. Having done this, members can feel more confident that the work is being performed as planned and that members will not get in each other's way or repeat what has already been done.

Clarifying roles can be motivational, especially if members set personal goals for fulfilling their roles. For example, if your team is writing a technical report together, and each member is assigned a chapter, you might set the personal goal of finishing your chapter by next Friday. Such a goal can energize you, while helping you to develop a strategy for meeting it. In order to meet this goal, you might plan to finish the outline by tomorrow, then write from this outline, then go back and smooth out the draft, and so on.

A perennial problem on teams is that members' personal goals appear to conflict with team goals. Members are encouraged to put the team's interests above their own. On healthy teams, however, personal and team goals are aligned.

For example, the desire for career advancement—promotions, more money, status and power within the organization—can conflict with the goals of the team, but it doesn't have to. If you pursue advancement by trampling over teammates, taking credit for their work, or barricading yourself in your office to produce brilliant work on your own—then this goal effectively competes with the goals of your team. Yet, if you pursue advancement by helping teammates, providing brilliant ideas for their benefit, or keeping the team focused on the mission, then career advancement can be in harmony with team goals. Eventually, people will notice and reward your contribution. This is especially true in healthy teams, where collaboration is valued.

A second common personal goal is to create innovative, high-quality, interesting work. Again, you can try to be creative and brilliant in the sterile confines of your office, but you are more likely to succeed if you work with your team to achieve this goal. Team settings provide stimulation and feedback needed to produce brilliant results.

A third common personal goal is to have good friends, satisfying relationships, and a supportive, enjoyable work environment. This goal, of course, can be pursued simultaneously with the pursuit of your team's goals. Healthy teams can fulfill our need for community.

So it is possible for members to work toward the overall goals of the team while also striving for personal goals such as earning promotions, producing innovative work, and having satisfying relationships. It's just a matter of finding ways to fit one's goals with those of the team.

Ways to Help

Set personal goals. Some, but not all, of your goals will be the same as your team's goals. The most beneficial goals are those that are: (1) specific— for example, "Sell 125% of my quota" as opposed to "Sell like crazy"; (2) challenging—based on the maximum of what you feel you are capable of doing; (3) meaningful—resulting in valued outcomes, such as pride or job security; and (4) measurable—you should know how close you are to achieving your goals or at least be certain when they are attained.

Organize goals into short-term, covering a day or two; medium-term, covering a month or two; and long-term, extending out a few years. Short-term goals help you be productive each day, medium-term goals help you get projects finished, and long-term goals help you aim your life in the desired direction.

Identify goals that conflict with team goals. Be honest about this one. If you do have such personal goals, you will need either to give them up, live with the conflict, or find ways to reformulate them so they fit with team goals.

Keep goals alive. Share them with other members or the leader. Review goals periodically to check progress. Set new goals when the old ones have been attained or are no longer motivating to you.

Ask teammates for elaboration on your role. Tell them how you view your job, and ask whether they agree and what else they would add.

Write a statement of your purpose. It does not necessarily have to be formal, only an accurate reflection of the role you believe you should play on the team.

Chapter 11

Empowering Yourself and Teammates

On its next adventure, Team Fantastic is transported to New York City on a hot August afternoon in the 1990s. Someone opened the wrong water valve, sending three times the normal pressure down a major pipeline. As a result, the pipe has broken in several different places on a busy street and numerous tall office buildings are without water. The team's mission: Repair the leaks before rush hour.

Fixing water leaks would appear to require a variety of skills, such as the ability to operate a jackhammer, tractor, shovel, and welder. It also requires knowledge of the procedures for blocking traffic and protecting the safety of the work crew, as well as the ability to inspect the work to ensure that it is all done to standard.

If the team were a normal work crew, you might assign one person to drive the tractor, one to work the jackhammer, one to do the welding, one to use the shovel, and another to direct traffic. You would also probably require that an inspector or two be present to ensure that each step of the job is done properly. Perhaps this explains why we often see four people watching while one person works on the street or why street problems can take so long to be fixed.

With all due respect for the regulations that repair crews must follow, Team Fantastic has no intention of providing a spectacle of inefficient teamwork. You did it once when only the ducks were watching by the lake and are determined to avoid it now that you are surrounded by angry motorists.

Because you are a fantastic team, each member has learned to perform all of these tasks (driving the tractor, working the jackhammer, welding, and so on). Having learned to look for tools that would be helpful to the team, one member says, "Hey, we have access to several sets of equipment." Another person says, "Right, we can each play several roles and divide the team up so that just a couple of people can work on each leak. That way we can work on all the leaks simultaneously and get them fixed by rush hour."

Crews of two go to each leak. One person operates the jackhammer, then the tractor, then uses the shovel to expose the pipe, cuts the pipe with a torch, and welds a replacement piece in place. Meanwhile, the second person directs traffic and occasionally switches roles to give the first person a breather. Then they take turns inspecting the pipe before the hole is filled with dirt. No one else and no other inspection is needed. As a result, the team, working simultaneously on all of the leaks, accomplishes its mission: Water is restored to the high-rises, and all lanes are reopened before rush hour.

Anyone who has started a business from scratch knows that this story of an empowered, multitalented team is not so far-fetched. In small, hungry companies, everybody plays multiple roles and everyone has to be trusted to do the work right. In larger, established companies, such teams are rare, however.

The key to the success of Team Fantastic in this instance is that all members are empowered to do the work that needs to be done. *Empowerment* means different things to different people. Literally, it means "giving power to." Empowerment requires a successful partnership between team leader and member. For the member's part, he or she must prove to be a reliable, resourceful, and multitalented employee. For the leader's part, he or she must give subordinates opportunities to learn new skills and prove themselves. The leader must also be willing and able to relinquish control, a formidable challenge for those who have been rewarded for keeping control and who have learned to trust only themselves to do the job right. Of course the organization also plays a role in empowering a team, giving members significant responsibility and opportunities to develop new skills.

Empowerment is important because individuals need the freedom to use their gifts for the benefit of their team. If members must always ask for permission, if they are expected—either implicitly or explicitly—to limit their attention to one small part of the work, they will not be able to fully employ their skills, experience, and other talents. In short, empowered teams get more done because more members are trusted and capable of doing the work.

Ways the Leader Can Empower Others

Give members opportunities to learn and develop so you will feel confident in giving them more responsibility in the future. Some leaders set their subordinates up for failure by giving them responsibilities that are above their ability. Instead, allow members to work on projects that you think they can handle, and continue to increase the complexity as long as you feel they stand a good chance of succeeding. Give them adequate guidance and follow up with them from time to time to see how they are doing. Ultimately, as they become more skilled, you will develop more trust in them and therefore be able to give them more responsibility.

Ask members to suggest ways to improve how your team does its work. If you are used to being in charge and doing things your own way, you may need to add "What do you suggest?" to your repertoire of frequently asked questions. When you receive suggestions, be prepared to respond by implementing at least part of what is suggested. People hate being asked for their opinion and then having it be ignored.

Model an openness to criticism. When someone on your team disagrees with you, demonstrate your openness by saying, "Tell me a little more about why you say that," then listen to the response without immediately passing judgment. If you are opinionated and generally firm in your beliefs, this may be tough for you, but the rewards will be that members will feel more listened to and will speak up when they disagree.

Ways Members Can Earn Empowerment

Take steps to earn the trust of the people who can give you more control over your work. Set a personal goal to establish a reputation as someone whom your leader or organization can trust to get the work done.

Ask the organization or leader for greater authority on a specific, manageable task. Then work your way up to having authority over more important or challenging tasks.

Scan the horizon for team problems within your scope of control. Solve them to demonstrate your initiative and problem-solving mentality.

Avoid chronic complainers. Those who constantly complain are seldom given more power or freedom. If you have no choice but to work with complainers, resist the temptation to join in the complaining.

Chapter 12

Reviewing the Past

A time machine comes in handy when you want to review team performance. You don't have to rely on your memory, view a videotape, or analyze memos written by your teammates. You can simply travel back in time, go to where your team was, and watch yourselves at work. In its next adventure, this is exactly what Team Fantastic does: It goes back in time and watches itself in action.

First it travels back to the jungle and observes from the bushes. As you watch yourselves roam the terrain, one team member whispers, "I like how we were so focused, so committed to surviving as a team." Another member adds, "I like how we all put our skills to good use." A third person whispers, "Look at how we all huddled for a moment to talk about our strategy. That really kept us out of trouble."

Then the team travels back to the moon, where you hide behind a large rock and watch yourselves at work. One person remarks, "I like the way we learned to use our time more efficiently on the moon, especially the way we held those short meetings to plan ahead." Another member adds, "Yeah, we really learned from our early mistakes."

Next, you travel back to the time you rode the bicycle around the lake and you watch yourselves in action. One member remarks, "Boy, at first we were so poorly coordinated it was almost comical." Another adds, "Yeah, we selected John to drive the bike because he was a good cyclist and that was important, but we also needed to talk through the process for stopping or starting the bike before we even got on." A third person adds, "You know, the way we kept falling down, it's a miracle that we never got in a fight. It's a good thing that we have all learned to trust each other and to focus on getting the work done!"

Finally, you travel back to the busy street in New York City. One person remarks, "I like how we developed multiple talents and that we were trusted to go out and do the job on our own. We would never have accomplished that mission without dividing the team up the way we did."

You all agree that you have done some things well and some poorly. But knowing this is not enough: Your experiences of the past must be distilled into lessons for the future. Someone on the team says, "Okay, so we've done some things right and some wrong in the past. What does this imply about what we should start doing, stop doing, or continue doing in the future?"

Although your teammates are hard-pressed to come up with actions that the team should stop doing in the future, they do have ideas about what they should start or continue to do. For example:

"Let's continue to focus on the work so we don't let conflict get in our way."

"Let's continue to hold brief meetings to keep everybody informed."

"Let's continue to assess our skills and make sure everybody is able to use their special talents."

"Let's start talking more about strategy before we jump into a new task, like riding that darned bicycle."

Another example of constructive team assessment is the reviewing of game films by athletic teams. Sports teams spend hours reviewing their performance and looking for ways to improve. They watch the films in slow-motion, backwards, forwards, and stop-frame to identify what they did right or wrong. Ideally, each player uses the lessons of the game to develop a plan for what he or she should do differently or the same in the next game.

Unfortunately, business teams rarely engage in such reflection. One reason is that they are too busy. Unlike sports teams or music groups, business teams are *always* performing in some way, so spending time on reflection requires stealing time from the immediate tasks at hand. A second reason is that they lack records such as video- or audiotape (or a time machine) to help them review their performance. Third, and perhaps most important, some teams are afraid to be openly critical of what they have done. Criticizing others requires tact and candor; accepting criticism requires a healthy ego and a willingness to improve. Such qualities are not universal. Yet teams can learn only when they are willing and able to review and encapsulate the lessons of the past.

Ways to Help

Set aside a time to discuss lessons of the past. This might be after a major deadline or at least once each year during a retreat. When planning a task, add one final step: task review. If you don't set the time aside, your team is likely to rush ahead to the next challenge without learning from the last one.

Develop action plans for team improvement. As a team, make a list with these parts: (1) what we should start doing, (2) what we should stop doing, and (3) what we should continue doing right. Be specific about who is responsible for carrying out these plans. Put the plan in writing and distribute

it to the members. (See chapter 19—"Turning Ideas into Action"— for more specific suggestions.)

Use a standardized team-measurement instrument. Such an instrument gathers feedback from members and people outside your team, such as customers, who are in a good position to evaluate the team. The results can stimulate a focused discussion about what the team does well or poorly. Re-administer the survey every six months to a year or at least revisit some of the issues raised by the survey.

Watch what other teams do; learn from their experience. While the dumb team repeats mistakes and the smart team learns from them, the wise team learns from other teams' mistakes (and successes).

Seek feedback. See chapter 14—"Giving and Receiving Feedback"— for more on this topic.

Chapter 13

Becoming More Innovative

In reflecting upon the successes and failures of the past, Team Fantastic realizes that each member has offered interesting, creative solutions to problems. On the moon, one member volunteered to monitor and record information from NASA, and the team gathered each day to listen to the recording rather than being bombarded all day with intermittent messages. In the jungle one member concocted a bug repellent from hairspray and lemon juice. At the park someone suggested that the team get off the bike and practice going though the motions of getting on and off an imaginary bike, so the team could rehearse without getting hurt. Each of these innovations has paid off.

In summary, one person says, "I really like how we are innovative when faced with challenges. Let's continue to do that in the future." Being innovative is important on just about any team. And just about anyone can be creative. It doesn't require that you paint, write poetry, play music, or make movies. Rather, being innovative simply means seeking and finding different and better ways to do the work. It means offering new and valuable ideas.

Of course some professions do allow less creativity than others. Try to be creative as an accountant and you are likely to get yourself put in jail. Still, most vocations do require innovation. We have reached a period of history in which organizations that are comfortable resting on their laurels are likely to perish. Almost every product we buy looks different from the one we bought just a few years ago. Cars have air bags, homes have electronic thermostats, bicycles have shock absorbers, computers have CD-ROMs, and stockbrokers sell a whole variety of newfangled financial products. It's hard to compete if your cars or computers don't have the latest features.

Unwritten rules about innovation are important. "Do it the way it has always been done" may be the rule that guides your team. Or, through the example of the team leader or other innovative members, your team may have developed the unwritten (perhaps even written) rule, "Push the envelope of creativity every day." Which rule guides your team?

Ways to Help

Seek exposure to stimulating people and ideas outside the team. Arrange to meet outside experts whose work is novel in some way. Go to

trade conferences or hire a consultant to tell you how other teams may be accomplishing the same work in a novel way.

Obtain technology to enhance creativity. A tool such as a new camera, electronic gadget, or software package can give members power to innovate.

Allow time for free discussion of ideas without evaluation. Hold brainstorming sessions. Ask for creative solutions to a specific problem. Suspend criticism until the team has generated as many ideas as possible, then examine the merits of these ideas.

Reward creative achievements. For example, give out trophies that are shaped like light bulbs for the "bright idea" award.

Strive to reduce the penalty for failure. Absorb the risks taken by your teammates. If a superior reprimands you because a teammate tried something new and failed, consider saying, "Yes, that's right; I'm sorry it turned out that way, but I commend my teammate for having the courage to try a new approach. That's the price we pay for being innovative. In the long run I think it will pay off."

As a team, identify and address barriers to innovation. Is money the problem? Not enough time? Not enough empowerment from top management? Fear of failure? Fear of having to work too hard? Just plain fear of change? Work to overcome these barriers. Perhaps the first place to apply creativity is in working around these perceived barriers.

One way to initiate such a discussion is to say to your team, "In a perfect world, where we would have all the time, freedom, or money we could ever need, what would we do differently?" Once team members respond to this question, ask them, "Well, what specifically is holding us back?" Then ask, "Okay, of those barriers, which ones can we do something about and what are we prepared to do to overcome them?"

Constantly experiment with small improvements. Small changes that involve minimal risks can add up to sizable improvements that can be highly rewarding. For example, if you compare the automobile of the twenties to modern automobiles the difference is striking. Still, the changes from year to year were usually minor. In much the same way, your product or service can continue to evolve so that in a few years from now it will look dramatically different.

Lead by example: Share your new ideas. For example, you might say to your team, "I'd like to share an idea I had that even I find to be slightly radical. In the spirit of creativity and innovation, I'd like you to consider it. Perhaps it will give us other ideas that we find even more valuable."

When faced with a new idea that has flaws, focus on what is good and novel about it and look for ways to make improvements. When someone comes up with a crazy idea your first reaction may be to say, "That's the most ridiculous idea I've ever heard" (and then, if you are the dramatic type, fall off your chair and break into laughter). If you want to encourage your teammates to continue to share their new ideas, however, you might say, "What I like about that idea is . . ." or, "That idea gets me thinking about yet another possibility . . . "

Chapter 14

Giving and Receiving Feedback

For its next adventure, Team Fantastic is transported to the green countryside of England on a lovely Saturday afternoon in the spring of 1683. You are standing behind a large stage constructed at the base of a grassy knoll. Each of you has a script in hand, and you are preparing for your next team mission: acting out a Shakespearean play before a crowd of several hundred people. So far, as you prepare to go on stage, everything is going fine—you have learned your lines and rehearsed the performance several times.

As you hear the audience arrive, you are filled with anticipation. You want to look just right for your acting debut. There is only one problem—as you don your costume and apply your makeup, you realize that you have no mirrors. You have no way to see if your hair is brushed or combed right, and you're not absolutely positive that your costume really goes together. For all you know, you may look like you just woke up. Yet you are expected to go on stage looking confident.

If you would feel uneasy in this situation, ask yourself this: Why is it that we have become so dependent on our ability to evaluate our appearance in the mirror, yet we can go for months without seeking feedback about how our team is viewed? Perhaps it is no surprise that some teams, in a figurative sense, have their shirts untucked and their hair sticking straight up. They rarely give themselves a good, honest look.

Team Fantastic is smart, though, so members help each other by providing constructive feedback: Chris, your collar is up on the right side; John, your hair is sticking up in the back; Sandra, your shirt is untucked on the side. Of course there is plenty of positive feedback as well, especially after these problems have been corrected. Having received this helpful feedback on your appearance, you can now stride confidently on stage knowing that you look good.

Teams need feedback both at the team level (e.g., about customer satisfaction) and at the individual level (e.g., about how you in particular are doing). Ongoing feedback helps the group learn and improve over time, so members can stride onto the stage of the real world feeling confident.

Ways to Help

Design a feedback system, such as regular customer interviews or surveys. Ask specific questions and encourage customers to be critical. Consider prefacing your customer-evaluation interview or survey with something like this: "Most people only say nice things about us and that's fine, but we want some good solid, critical feedback that we can use to make real improvements in the future. Remember, your responses are confidential."

If you send out customer-evaluation surveys, follow up with a phone call or another letter to stress how important their feedback is. Even if you do not receive helpful feedback, you can at least demonstrate a concern for your customer's opinions.

Study the feedback you receive, looking for trends and specific ways to improve. Translate the feedback into actions that you and your team can take to better meet the needs of your customers.

Ask teammates for their honest feedback. Tell them what topics you want feedback on. For example, you could say, "Chris, as one of my teammates, your opinion is important to me. Give it to me straight: When it comes to working with the other team members, what do you think I'm good at and in what areas can I improve? How about my technical skills? What are my strengths and what skills do you suggest I develop?"

Affirm members for what they do well. Positive feedback is as important as criticism and often more helpful. Here's an exercise for a team retreat. Ask members to stand and roam the room as if at a cocktail party. Have each member tell each teammate what talent, strength, or contribution that teammate has to offer. Although this experience may seem touchy-feely to you, you are likely to remember what your teammates tell you and to continue doing what they say you're doing right.

Accept criticism without defending yourself. Criticism can of course be difficult to accept. The natural reaction is to argue back or diminish the criticism in some way. A healthy reaction to critical feedback is to say, "It's tough to hear that kind of criticism, but you have a point and I'll think about what you have said." If you react defensively you cut yourself off from useful feedback in the future and often make yourself look worse.

Give feedback without making a mountain out of a molehill. In an effort to avoid hurting our teammates' feelings, offending them, or losing our jobs, we can make a bigger deal out of giving feedback than we need to. If a teammate needs critical feedback, state it as simple fact rather than a momentous crisis that must be solved. If Bob, your teammate, sends out memos that are full of typos, you might be tempted to start by saying, "Bob, you've got a problem that I need to tell you about" or, "I need to give you

some feedback." Once you have said this, however, Bob will likely feel threatened, nervous, and react defensively to the feedback. Rather, you might say, "Bob, do you realize your last memo had nine typos in it?"

Give feedback in the spirit of partnership. For example, you might go on to say to Bob, "I'm afraid if your memos have typos, people will focus on your typos rather than the great ideas you present."

Focus on the behavior rather than the person. For example, rather than telling Jim that he is insensitive and rude, call his attention to what he does, such as interrupting other people when they are in midsentence. Say, "Jim, do you realize that you interrupted Chris five times when he was talking?"

Make giving and receiving feedback a regular part of teamwork. Giving feedback can seem risky; the natural reaction is to avoid it for fear of offending the person or jeopardizing your career. Still, the more you avoid it, the harder it is to do. Conversely, the more you do it, the less risky it will seem.

Call your human resources or personnel director to ask about training programs on giving and receiving feedback. Look for courses that give you an opportunity to practice these skills (not just hear a lecture about them).

Develop warm relationships with your teammates so that you can trust each other to offer helpful feedback in a spirit of goodwill. Criticism is easier to give and receive when both of you are confident that it is offered in a sincere desire to help. (See chapter 9—"Managing Conflict.")

Chapter 15

Rewarding Performance

Team Fantastic's makeup and costumes were just right, and, for a bunch of rookies, you put on a pretty good show. When the play is over and you all come out to take a bow, you receive rousing applause. How good it feels to be appreciated.

Imagine how it would feel to have the audience just stand in silence. No cheers, no applause, not even a single person clapping. How disappointing this would feel.

It goes without saying that most of us live for rewards. We don't need people clapping for us all the time, nor do we need to be handed cash every day. But we need to feel that we are valued, that what we are doing is important and appreciated. Yet in some organizations today, effective performance is met with silence. No clapping, not even a little acknowledgment.

If you are in such an organization, in the long run you may wonder whether the work is really worth it, just as the members of Team Fantastic would wonder whether putting on the play was worth it if no one clapped.

Rewards serve many purposes: to motivate, to make people feel valued and supported, and to provide feedback on what people are doing right; when rewards are withheld, it conveys, albeit indirectly, the idea that the person is doing something wrong.

One obvious form of reward is money, but in most organizations members can't go around handing out cash to each other when they do a good job; the most one can expect is an occasional bonus check. Fortunately, there are other types of rewards that many people find equally or more rewarding than money: human affirmation—a pat on the back, note of thanks, or simple smile at the right moment. In most teams, people have a wealth of such gifts to give, but they sometimes neglect to give them away. Members can become so preoccupied with the task at hand that they neglect to utter the mere two words, "Good job."

As a member of your team, you have deep pockets filled with praise and affirmation ready to be given away. It may be time for you to think about how you can share these rewards with your teammates, so that their achievements are not met with silence.

Ways the Leader or Prominent Member Can Help

Publicly praise members when they perform well. For example, say to your team, "Hey, let's give Julie a hand for the excellent job she did in the presentation," or, "Sarah, I noticed that you have really taken initiative on this project. We all appreciate it."

Reflect on whether you are sending the right signals to your team. When your top performers work their tails off, do you "reward" them by giving them more responsibility, making them work longer hours? The last time your team came up with a great innovation or worked throughout the night to fix a problem or to meet a deadline, did you publicly acknowledge their effort or did you take credit for the good work they did? When one of your teammates drops the ball, do you reward that person by giving him or her fewer responsibilities? Your reactions to high or low performance can have unintended results.

Find out what motivates your teammates. Some people like to be challenged; some work better with frequent praise; others like to be able to see visible results. You probably can make assumptions about what motivates the members of your team, but do you really know?

One way to learn more about what motivates your teammates is to ask them to tell you about a time when they felt most excited about their work. Why did they feel so motivated? A more formal method is to conduct the following exercise in a retreat setting. List ten values that you think are motivating to at least some of your team members. For example, some of these values might be financial security, social recognition, close interpersonal relationships, helping others, professional challenge, seeing the results of the work, and getting rich. Ask each member to rank the importance of these values to them. Open a discussion with the rest of your team by sharing your own rankings.

Target rewards to teammates' needs and desires. Experiment with several different types of rewards to see which ones seem to be most valued.

Make others aware of your team successes. For example, write progress reports that document the wonderful work that your team has accomplished. Share this report with your team. Not only will this serve to build organizational support, as discussed in chapter 4, but it will also affirm your teammates for their contributions.

Help your team recognize modest milestones, not just the major triumphs. People sometimes become so immersed in immediate demands that they fail to acknowledge their little successes. You might say, "Hey, folks, we just finished a terrific month; look at these month-end figures. Let's treat ourselves to lunch at a nice restaurant!"

Ways All Members Can Help

Catch your teammate doing something well. Give your teammate a compliment, such as, "I noticed you did a really creative job with that brochure. Way to go, Susan." Saying "good job" requires a mere two words, yet these words can be exactly what someone needs to hear.

Follow the four-to-one rule. For every time you punish or criticize your teammates, try to praise them at least four times.

Stop and smell the roses. Often members become so immersed in their own work that they overlook the great work that their teammates are doing. Take time to remove yourself from your work and look at what the people around you are doing. Find in each of your teammates at least one quality that is worthy of praise.

Call attention to your contributions. If you have done something outstanding and no one has seemed to notice, ask your teammates, "Well, how did you like what I did?" Sometimes they will not notice unless you call a little attention to what you have done; often they might have thought a compliment without verbalizing it.

Chapter 16

Leading the Team

After these challenges, if a Martian were to come to Earth and say to Team Fantastic, "Take me to your leader," you would probably have to give this somewhat confusing response: "I am the leader. So is he. So is she. In fact, we all act as leaders from time to time."

Indeed, one person led in the jungle, another person led on the bike, and you all seemed to lead on the streets of New York City. It really didn't matter who the formal leader was because you all pitched in, took responsibility for leading the team, and ensured that the work got done. As members become more skilled and trusting of each other, leadership can be shared like this and all members take some responsibility for leadership.

Still, most teams do have one leader, who often possesses important political skills, experience, and organizational knowledge. The leader, with help from the members, bears primary responsibility for the following tasks:

(1) Communicating a vision—a clear, meaningful, and evolving vision of the team's mission. This would also include setting standards for excellence and working with the team to set specific goals.

(2) Keeping the team organized—making certain that members know what they are supposed to do and are communicating and planning well so that time, effort, and other resources are not wasted; making certain that everyone's skills and knowledge are fully utilized.

(3) Helping the team learn and grow—guiding members into challenging but manageable assignments; seeking information about what the team is doing right or wrong; giving constructive feedback to individual members; and providing psychological or emotional support for them.

(4) Pursuing needed resources such as money, tools, office space, information, and opportunity. This requires representing the team well to outside constituencies and paying attention to politics.

What needs to be stressed, however, is that all members should contribute in these areas. All members can help clarify a team's vision, keep things organized, help it learn and grow, and pursue needed resources.

Ways the Leader Can Develop Team Leadership Skills

Get to know someone who has a reputation as an effective team leader. Take that person out to lunch and ask how he or she does it. Ask for that person's help as a mentor or supporter in the effort to be a better team leader.

Seek professional feedback and training in team leadership. Training courses and multi-rater feedback instruments for team leaders are available. Consult your human resources department for suggestions of individuals or organizations that offer these services.

Seek out other resources about team leadership. Videotapes and in-house training programs may be available through your human resources or personnel department.

Pursue improvements in the other areas discussed in this book. This may mean working with members to clarify the team mission (see chapter 7—"Clarifying the Mission"), encouraging members with different opinions to express their ideas (see chapter 11—"Empowering Yourself and Teammates"), praising or otherwise rewarding members when they perform well (see chapter 15—"Rewarding Performance"), and striving to obtain tools and other necessary resources (see chapter 3—"Exploring Team Tools").

Ways the Member Can Help the Leader

Make contributions in areas where the leader has weaknesses. If the leader rarely has encouraging words for teammates, help by praising and otherwise supporting them. If the leader is disorganized, volunteer to keep a team schedule or to occasionally hold meetings in the leader's absence.

Be an effective team representative in interactions with its constituencies. Every member can be a team ambassador. Accept and play that role enthusiastically.

Tell the leader about opportunities to learn more about team leadership. Give the leader this book, point out other books and videos that are available, or pass along brochures on team-leadership training programs.

Chapter 17

Enjoying the Team Experience

If someone were to ask, "How was your experience as a member of Team Fantastic?" you would probably say something like, "It was terrific. I really enjoyed it." Or, if it didn't go so well for you, you might say, "It was dreadful. I thought it would never end!" You might recount the mistakes the team made or its achievements, but the odds are good that you would also touch upon whether you enjoyed it. This seems to be human nature: Enjoyment matters, even if the bottom line is whether the team meets its goals, turns a profit, and satisfies its customers.

Enjoyment can be important for the bottom line as well. Team members have to be ready and willing to work together effectively in the future. And they have to bring a positive attitude to each new team they join. Thus, it is usually important—both to the members and to the bottom line—that people enjoy being on a team.

How can you and your teammates enjoy your team more? This is a complex topic, not easily addressed in a few pages. Much of our happiness stems from factors that are out of the control of the leader or other members, such as our biological (chemical) makeup, our past experiences that have established our expectations, and our lives outside of work. Still, there are ways to form an environment in which team members will tend to enjoy themselves.

Ways to Help

Explore what makes your teammates happy or unhappy. Ask, "When were you the happiest? Why were you happy at that time?" The answers may help you contribute to a satisfying team environment.

Ask unhappy members what is bothering them. For example, "Chris, I noticed you have been frowning a lot lately. What's up? How can I help?" Perhaps Chris feels unappreciated, thinks his career is going nowhere, feels underpaid, or is irritated by the way he is being treated by the other team members. You may not be able to do anything about it, but at least you can show your concern and you will know what is wrong.

Redesign the work so members find their tasks more interesting and meaningful. Members tend to be most fulfilled when they have an opportunity to use a variety of skills, be responsible for a whole project from start to

finish, see the results of their work, and receive direct feedback from customers.

Praise your teammates when they deserve it and compliment them on their strengths. See chapter 15—"Rewarding Performance"—for more suggestions in this area.

Relax when you are working with your team. If you are unhappy when working together, it may mean that you are just too tense. There are many ways to relax, some pretty obvious, others a little far out. Before going into a team meeting, close your eyes and pretend that you are in a soothing place such as a sandy beach in the tropics. Or think about some of the jokes you heard the last time you listened to a comedian. Try taking a few deep breaths and letting the air out very slowly. Pretend that the air flowing from your lungs represents the troubles that you have kept locked inside. Or exercise in the morning or at lunch time so you will feel more relaxed the rest of the day.

If you are witty, use good, clean humor to loosen up the team. Funny people can bless even the most depressed team with moments of levity.

Smile. If you walk around with a frown on your face (either because you are unhappy or because for you smiling takes a lot of work), you give off the signal that you don't want to be around other people. Frowning can have the same effect on your teammates as bug repellent has on mosquitoes: They stay away.

Take responsibility for your happiness. We are in an age when it is accepted, indeed popular, to blame others for our own problems. Rather than blaming others, ask yourself to what extent you currently add to the problems of the team. Have you been dissatisfied on other teams? If you are part of the problem, you may be part of the solution.

Explore whether you or others suffer from depression. Symptoms of severe depression include loss of appetite and sex drive and changes in sleep patterns (sleeping either more or less than usual). Those who suffer from depression should seek help from a qualified mental-health professional.

Pursue solutions in the other areas discussed in this book. Being disorganized, having an unclear mission, competing with each other—these are all possible causes of dissatisfaction. Be proactive about solving these other problems and you might soon find yourself or your teammates happier to be part of the team.

Chapter 18

Focusing on Performance

With all of this discussion about feedback, rewards, team assessment, gathering resources, and so on, one might wonder where team performance comes into play. After all, teams exist to perform. Aren't these other activities just a distraction from performance, a waste of time?

No, they are not a waste of time. Such tasks are as important to the performance of the team as changing the oil is to the performance of an automobile. In fact, teams have become known as the "Ferrari" of organizations: high performance but also high maintenance. In addition to changing the oil of a Ferrari, the owner needs to keep it well-tuned, make frequent repairs, feed it with lots of high-octane fuel—all this costs money and time. But when the "rubber hits the road," the car can leave others in a plume of smoke.

Teams are the same way. They can produce tremendous results if they are well-maintained. This means attending to issues such as feedback, rewards, team assessment, and gathering resources.

Team performance is not just about speed, however. Performance can mean meeting team objectives, doing high-quality work, making a difference in the world, satisfying the customer, gaining market share, or all of the above. Teams that focus myopically on just one aspect of performance run the risk of failing in other ways.

Similarly, teams that focus on present performance may overlook the important task of building for future performance. One might argue that Team Fantastic wasn't fantastic at all. Members wasted oxygen on the moon and crashed the bicycle, for instance. What made the team fantastic was not just what it achieved in the present but what it learned from these experiences that will make it fantastic in the future.

Although all of the ideas presented in this book can help the team improve its performance, I'll emphasize a few key ideas that are most likely to boost the performance of your Ferrari.

Ways to Help

Set clear goals. See chapter 7—"Clarifying the Mission"—and chapter 10—"Clarifying Personal Goals." As mentioned in these chapters, goals can have a powerful effect on the performance of your team. A team without clear goals is like a traveler without a destination; both are prone to wander without making progress.

Seek honest feedback. See chapter 14—"Giving and Receiving Feedback." A team without feedback is like a traveler who is never sure he or she is going in the right direction.

Build the team's skills. See chapter 5—"Building and Utilizing Skills." In particular, define the skills requirements for your team, and either hire members with the needed skills or pursue training opportunities.

Even in the absence of problems, address other challenges discussed in this book: managing the time crunch; handling the information load; getting the resources your team needs; getting support from your organization; building member commitment; developing better coordination; managing conflict; empowering yourself and your teammates; reviewing your team's performance; becoming more innovative as a team; giving and receiving feedback; rewarding performance; leading your team well; and helping team members be happy.

Team performance stems from many sources. The more strengths you have in all of the areas covered in this book, the better your team will perform and the more you will enjoy being part of it.

Chapter 19

Turning Ideas Into Action

The recommendations given here cannot be turned into action overnight. Helping your team will require an ongoing process of reflection, exploration, involvement, and then action. *Reflect* upon your team and how you fit in; *explore* how others see the team and your role as a member or leader; *involve* your teammates in the process of change; and take *action*. In healthy teams, this cycle is ongoing:

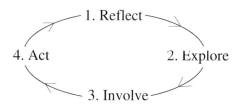

Reflect

As you reflect upon your team and your role on this team, at least three questions are important to consider:

First, how is your team doing? What does it do well or poorly? What parts of this book seem to most directly address its current needs? More specifically, are members committed? Is the mission clear? Is your team well-organized? Is it sufficiently empowered so members are both able and allowed to do work in the absence of the leader?

Second, are you committed to helping your team? Are you willing and able to reflect honestly on your shortcomings as a team member or leader? Do you want to be a team player or would you prefer to be more independent? Do you believe you can make a difference in your team? Are you willing to follow through with the commitments that you make? Are you willing to state your commitments publicly? Is there anything that prevents you from trying to help your team?

Third, how can you best contribute to your team in the future? What unique skills, abilities, or experience do you possess that can benefit the team? Which actions listed in this book would you like to take (or do more often) to help the team in the near future?

The worksheet at the end of this chapter lists the recommendations for action that have been presented in each chapter. To help you reflect on your

team and your place in it, read through these and check the ten or fifteen that you find most valuable. (You can make a photocopy of the worksheet if you would prefer not to write in this book.) The ones that you select should address a clear need, be worth the effort, and be likely to be supported by your teammates.

Once you have selected the ten or fifteen most useful recommendations, then go back and try to identify the top two or three. Rewrite these as specific and measurable goals. For example:

"Within the next two months, I will develop a new system for collecting specific feedback from our important customers."

"Starting next week, I will begin our weekly meetings with 'Before we jump into the rest of the business, let's take time to share what is going well on the team.'"

"Once a day, I will say hello to at least one other team member and take a few minutes to see what he or she is doing and how I can help."

Explore

Having reflected upon your team and set some tentative goals for helping it, you will find it useful to explore several issues with your teammates. How do they view your team? What do they see as your strengths and shortcomings as a team member or leader? Do they think that your goals for helping your team are realistic? Input from others will ensure that you are on the right track.

Reading this book as a team will provide members with common metaphors for teamwork. If all of the members read it, you will be able to generate discussion with questions such as the following:

Which adventure strikes us as most relevant to this team and why? Would our team have survived these adventures? If not, which adventure would have been our demise?

Do we need to go down the railroad track to explore other technologies? Are there other teams that are laying more track because they have better tools or equipment?

Do we need to take a time-out in the jungle to make sure we are clear about our roles? What snakes or headhunters threaten us? What are the supplies (the resources and other support) that we need from our organization to survive this jungle?

Do we need to communicate more clearly and better coordinate our efforts to avoid crashing our bicycle? Have we crashed in the past? What tasks will we be doing in the future that resemble riding the long bicycle? What information will need to be conveyed to all of the riders to ensure we don't crash or fall off?

Involve

By exploring these issues with your team, you take the crucial step of involving them in the effort to improve its functioning. Involvement, however, also means getting your teammates to work with you. It will be much easier for you to make changes if your teammates are also changing, and if they make a commitment to support you in the improvement effort.

There are several ways to involve your team. For example, ask each member to select two or three recommendations for action from this book that he or she would like to set goals around. Invite members to share their goals with the other members. Using the worksheet, check off the ones that have been selected by at least one member, then have your team read through the list, looking for areas in which improvement is needed but no one has selected an item. Ask for volunteers to select additional items, if necessary.

Once each member has set several goals, it will be helpful to create "coaching pairs"—pairs of team members who make a commitment to help each other follow through with their plans. Your partner can help you further clarify your commitments and give you ongoing feedback on whether you appear to be "walking your talk." You in turn can help your partner do the same. Post your goals in a central place so that you, your partner, and other teammates are reminded of your commitments. Select a time and place when you and your partner will follow up on the progress each of you has made.

Act

Changing the way you view your team and increasing your awareness of its needs will be important but clearly not enough; the hard part is behaving differently in observable ways. You may need to perform a behavior repeatedly before it is noticed or has an effect on your team. Follow the Nike™ motto, with one modification: Just do it . . . over and over again. Whatever you vow to do differently, try to make it a practice rather than a one-shot effort.

In summary, if you reflect, explore, involve, and then act, you will be on the road to a more productive and healthy team.

Worksheet
Improving Team Performance

Chapter 1: Managing the Time Crunch

1.1 ____ Prioritize team projects or responsibilities
1.2 ____ Drive productive meetings with pointed questions
1.3 ____ Count your minutes
1.4 ____ Be honest with callers about how much time you have to talk
1.5 ____ Study the accuracy of your planning predictions
1.6 ____ Avoid overcommitting yourself
1.7 ____ Prioritize the items on your to-do list
1.8 ____ If the team cannot accomplish the work in time, write a job description for selecting someone who could help
1.9 ____ Establish quality control procedures to catch mistakes that are likely to happen when your team is in a hurry
1.10 ____ Take steps to develop a more coordinated, efficient team

Chapter 2: Handling the Information Load

2.1 ____ Define the information needs of your team
2.2 ____ Divide information-gathering responsibilities among the members to minimize duplication of effort
2.3 ____ Ask each member to share important news in team meetings
2.4 ____ Make sure that minutes are distributed to all members, especially those who were unable to attend
2.5 ____ Take advantage of computer technology such as E-mail
2.6 ____ Develop routine reports for distributing repetitive, ongoing information
2.7 ____ Experiment with tracking mechanisms
2.8 ____ Identify and get to know specific individuals from whom you need important information
2.9 ____ Post frequently used data
2.10 ____ Use eye-catching methods to present information

Chapter 3: Exploring Team Tools

3.1 _____ Explore new technologies
3.2 _____ Write a "wish list"
3.3 _____ Prioritize the group's material needs
3.4 _____ Explore clever ways to obtain resources
3.5 _____ Develop a written justification for obtaining key resources to present to decision-makers
3.6 _____ Learn to use the equipment or tools that are now available

Chapter 4: Building Organizational Support

4.1 _____ Articulate the needs of your team
4.2 _____ Get to know leaders who can provide what your team needs
4.3 _____ Help others understand why it is important to support you
4.4 _____ Document and publicize your team's successes
4.5 _____ Ask for nonfinancial support such as training opportunities and feedback on the team's performance
4.6 _____ Show appreciation for the support you receive

Chapter 5: Building and Utilizing Skills

5.1 _____ Identify the critical skills and knowledge that spell the difference between average and superior team performance
5.2 _____ Learn more about your teammates' skills and experience
5.3 _____ For each of the skills or areas of knowledge that you think important to success, indicate who possesses it
5.4 _____ Seek out knowledge and opinions from the group, especially those who tend not to speak up
5.5 _____ Develop one new skill or area of knowledge
5.6 _____ Write a job description for a person who might fill your team's void in skill or knowledge
5.7 _____ Give other members guidance or tactful feedback when appropriate

Chapter 6: Building Commitment

6.1 _____ Write down what you believe to be the unwritten rules that guide the actions of your team

6.2 _____ Explicitly set new team norms

6.3 _____ Live the new team norms

6.4 _____ Assign well-defined tasks to specific individuals and hold them accountable

6.5 _____ Grant members more control over their work

6.6 _____ Give members the opportunity to perform a number of different activities to broaden their skills and perspectives

6.7 _____ Allow members to produce a whole and visible piece of work

6.8 _____ Introduce members to their constituents

6.9 _____ Minimize outside distractions

6.10 _____ Keep your team small

6.11 _____ Gather members together so they work in physical proximity, or at least provide ample opportunity for members to interact

6.12 _____ Set a positive example of commitment

Chapter 7: Clarifying the Mission

7.1 _____ Discuss the team's reason for being

7.2 _____ Write a brief statement of team purpose

7.3 _____ Set specific, achievable goals for the year

7.4 _____ Share your purpose or goals with important people outside the team

7.5 _____ Post a statement of your purpose and goals in your work area

7.6 _____ Seek clarification of how your current tasks fit the team mission

7.7 _____ Measure progress toward team goals

Chapter 8: Coordinating the Team

8.1 _____ Start tasks by discussing goals and strategy

8.2 _____ Assign work to individuals

8.3 _____ Organize short meetings to discuss the day or week ahead

8.4 _____ Choose a time and place to conduct long-range planning

8.5 _____ Set an example by planning ahead and keeping teammates informed about your activities

8.6 _____ Write an informal definition of your job and share it with other members

8.7 _____ Take steps to better handle your team's information load

Chapter 9: Managing Conflict

9.1 _____ Encourage members to switch perspectives

9.2 _____ Encourage open communication about each member's priorities

9.3 _____ Propose a modification of your team's performance appraisal system so that people are evaluated on how they handle conflict

9.4 _____ Select new, upbeat members who will have a positive impact on your team

9.5 _____ Participate in a team-development program

9.6 _____ Make "good news" an agenda item for team meetings

9.7 _____ Say hello to teammates and find out how they are doing

9.8 _____ Get to know teammates in a relaxed atmosphere

9.9 _____ Offer to help your teammates

9.10 _____ Care for your mental and physical health

9.11 _____ "Walk a mile in another's shoes" before finding fault or assigning blame

9.12 _____ Explain your actions before others invent their own explanations

9.13 _____ Focus on solutions without blaming others

9.14 _____ Avoid forming cliques to complain about problems

9.15 _____ Have a team member play the role of devil's advocate

9.16 _____ Divide your team into subgroups to reach independent decisions about a common question, then bring them back together to resolve differences

9.17 _____ Invite outside experts with different opinions

9.18 _____ Plan, on occasion, to have your team openly evaluate its strengths and weaknesses

Chapter 10: Clarifying Personal Goals

10.1 _____ Set personal goals

10.2 _____ Organize goals into short-, medium-, and long-term

10.3 _____ Identify goals that conflict with team goals

10.4 _____ Keep goals alive

10.5 _____ Ask teammates for elaboration on your role

10.6 _____ Write a statement of your purpose

Chapter 11: Empowering Yourself and Teammates

11.1 _____ Give members opportunities to learn and develop
11.2 _____ Ask members to suggest ways to improve how the team does its work
11.3 _____ Model an openness to criticism
11.4 _____ Earn the trust of people who can give you more control over your work
11.5 _____ Ask the organization or leader for greater authority on a specific, manageable task
11.6 _____ Scan the horizon for team problems within your scope of control
11.7 _____ Avoid chronic complainers

Chapter 12: Reviewing the Past

12.1 _____ Set aside a time to discuss lessons of the past
12.2 _____ Develop action plans for team improvement
12.3 _____ Use a standardized team-measurement instrument
12.4 _____ Watch what other teams do; learn from their experience
12.5 _____ Seek feedback

Chapter 13: Becoming More Innovative

13.1 _____ Seek exposure to stimulating people and ideas outside the team
13.2 _____ Obtain technology to enhance creativity
13.3 _____ Allow time for free discussion of ideas without evaluation
13.4 _____ Reward creative achievements
13.5 _____ Strive to reduce the penalty for failure
13.6 _____ As a team, identify and address barriers to innovation
13.7 _____ Constantly experiment with small improvements
13.8 _____ Lead by example: Share your new ideas
13.9 _____ With a new idea that has flaws, focus on what is good and look for ways to make improvements

Chapter 14: Giving and Receiving Feedback

14.1 _____ Design a feedback system, such as regular customer interviews or surveys

14.2 _____ Study the feedback you receive, looking for trends and specific ways to improve

14.3 _____ Ask teammates for their honest feedback

14.4 _____ Affirm members for what they do well

14.5 _____ Accept criticism without defending yourself

14.6 _____ Give feedback without making a mountain out of a molehill

14.7 _____ Give feedback in the spirit of partnership

14.8 _____ Focus on the behavior rather than the person

14.9 _____ Make giving and receiving feedback a regular part of teamwork

14.10_____ Ask your human resources director about training programs on giving and receiving feedback

14.11_____ Develop warm relationships with teammates in which you can offer feedback in a spirit of goodwill

Chapter 15: Rewarding Performance

15.1 _____ Publicly praise members when they perform well

15.2 _____ Reflect on whether you are sending the right signals to your team

15.3 _____ Find out what motivates your teammates

15.4 _____ Target rewards to teammates' needs and desires

15.5 _____ Make others aware of your team successes

15.6 _____ Help your team recognize modest milestones, not just major triumphs

15.7 _____ Catch your teammate doing something well

15.8 _____ Follow the four-to-one rule—four praises for each criticism

15.9 _____ Stop and smell the roses

15.10_____ Call attention to your contributions

Chapter 16: Leading the Team

16.1 _____ Get to know someone who has a reputation as an effective team leader

16.2 _____ Seek professional feedback and training in team leadership

16.3 _____ Seek other resources about team leadership

16.4 _____ Make contributions in areas where the leader has weaknesses

16.5 _____ Be an effective team representative in interactions with its constituencies

16.6 _____ Tell the leader about opportunities to learn more about team leadership

Chapter 17: Enjoying the Team Experience

17.1 _____ Explore what makes your teammates happy or unhappy

17.2 _____ Ask unhappy members what is bothering them

17.3 _____ Redesign the work so that members find their tasks more interesting and meaningful

17.4 _____ Praise teammates when they deserve it, and compliment them on their strengths

17.5 _____ Relax when you are working with your team

17.6 _____ If you are witty, use good, clean humor to loosen up the team

17.7 _____ Smile

17.8 _____ Take responsibility for your happiness

17.9 _____ Explore whether you or others suffer from depression

CENTER FOR CREATIVE LEADERSHIP PUBLICATIONS

SELECTED REPORTS:

The Adventures of Team Fantastic: A Practical Guide for Team Leaders and Members
G.L. Hallam (1996, Stock #172) $20.00
Beyond Work-Family Programs J.R. Kofodimos (1995, Stock #167) $25.00
CEO Selection: A Street-smart Review G.P. Hollenbeck (1994, Stock #164) $25.00
Coping With an Intolerable Boss M.M. Lombardo & M.W. McCall, Jr. (1984, Stock #305) $10.00
The Creative Opportunists: Conversations with the CEOs of Small Businesses
J.S. Bruce (1992, Stock #316) $12.00
Creativity in the R&D Laboratory T.M. Amabile & S.S. Gryskiewicz (1987, Stock #130) $12.00
The Dynamics of Management Derailment M.M. Lombardo & C.D. McCauley (1988, Stock #134). $12.00
Eighty-eight Assignments for Development in Place: Enhancing the Developmental
Challenge of Existing Jobs M.M. Lombardo & R.W. Eichinger (1989, Stock #136) $15.00
Enhancing 360-degree Feedback for Senior Executives: How to Maximize the Benefits and
Minimize the Risks R.E. Kaplan & C.J. Palus (1994, Stock #160) $15.00
An Evaluation of the Outcomes of a Leadership Development Program C.D. McCauley &
M.W. Hughes-James (1994, Stock #163) $35.00
Evolving Leaders: A Model for Promoting Leadership Development in Programs C.J. Palus &
W.H. Drath (1995, Stock #165) $20.00
Feedback to Managers, Volume I: A Guide to Evaluating Multi-rater Feedback Instruments
E. Van Velsor & J. Brittain Leslie (1991, Stock #149) $20.00
Feedback to Managers, Volume II: A Review and Comparison of Sixteen Multi-rater
Feedback Instruments E. Van Velsor & J. Brittain Leslie (1991, Stock #150) $80.00
Forceful Leadership and Enabling Leadership: You Can Do Both R.E. Kaplan (1996, Stock #171) $20.00
Gender Differences in the Development of Managers: How Women Managers Learn From
Experience E. Van Velsor & M. W. Hughes (1990, Stock #145) $35.00
A Glass Ceiling Survey: Benchmarking Barriers and Practices A.M. Morrison, C.T. Schreiber,
& K.F. Price (1995, Stock #161) $20.00
High Hurdles: The Challenge of Executive Self-development R.E. Kaplan, W.H. Drath, &
J.R. Kofodimos (1985, Stock #125) $15.00
The Intuitive Pragmatists: Conversations with Chief Executive Officers J.S. Bruce
(1986, Stock #310) $12.00
Key Events in Executives' Lives E.H. Lindsey, V. Homes, & M.W. McCall, Jr.
(1987, Stock #132) $65.00
Leadership for Turbulent Times L.R. Sayles (1995, Stock #325) $20.00
Learning How to Learn From Experience: Impact of Stress and Coping K.A. Bunker &
A.D. Webb (1992, Stock #154) $30.00
A Look at Derailment Today: North America and Europe J. Brittain Leslie & E. Van Velsor
(1996, Stock #169) $25.00
Making Common Sense: Leadership as Meaning-making in a Community of Practice
W.H. Drath & C.J. Palus (1994, Stock #156) $15.00
Managerial Promotion: The Dynamics for Men and Women M.N. Ruderman, P.J. Ohlott, &
K.E. Kram (1996, Stock #170) $15.00
Off the Track: Why and How Successful Executives Get Derailed M.W. McCall, Jr., &
M.M. Lombardo (1983, Stock #121) $10.00
Perspectives on Dialogue: Making Talk Developmental for Individuals and Organizations
N.M. Dixon (1996, Stock #168) $20.00
Preventing Derailment: What To Do Before It's Too Late M.M. Lombardo &
R.W. Eichinger (1989, Stock #138) $25.00
The Realities of Management Promotion M.N. Ruderman & P.J. Ohlott (1994, Stock #157) $20.00
Redefining What's Essential to Business Performance: Pathways to Productivity,
Quality, and Service L.R. Sayles (1990, Stock #142) $20.00
Succession Planning: An Annotated Bibliography L.J. Eastman (1995, Stock #324) $20.00
Training for Action: A New Approach to Executive Development R.M. Burnside &
V.A. Guthrie (1992, Stock #153) $15.00
Traps and Pitfalls in the Judgment of Executive Potential M.N. Ruderman & P.J. Ohlott
(1990, Stock #141) $20.00

Twenty-two Ways to Develop Leadership in Staff Managers R.W. Eichinger & M.M. Lombardo
(1990, Stock #144) $15.00
Upward-communication Programs in American Industry A.I. Kraut & F.H. Freeman
(1992, Stock #152) $30.00
Using an Art Technique to Facilitate Leadership Development C. De Ciantis (1995, Stock #166)... $30.00
Why Executives Lose Their Balance J.R. Kofodimos (1989, Stock #137) $20.00
Why Managers Have Trouble Empowering: A Theoretical Perspective Based on
Concepts of Adult Development W.H. Drath (1993, Stock #155) $15.00

SELECTED BOOKS:

Balancing Act: How Managers Can Integrate Successful Careers and Fulfilling Personal Lives
J.R. Kofodimos (1993, Stock #247) $27.00
Beyond Ambition: How Driven Managers Can Lead Better and Live Better R.E. Kaplan,
W.H. Drath, & J.R. Kofodimos (1991, Stock #227) $29.95
Breaking the Glass Ceiling: Can Women Reach the Top of America's Largest Corporations?
(Updated Edition) A.M. Morrison, R.P. White, & E. Van Velsor (1992, Stock #236A) $13.00
Choosing to Lead (Second Edition) K.E. Clark & M.B. Clark (1996, Stock #327) $25.00
Developing Diversity in Organizations: A Digest of Selected Literature A.M. Morrison &
K.M. Crabtree (1992, Stock #317) $25.00
Discovering Creativity: Proceedings of the 1992 International Creativity and Innovation
Networking Conference S.S. Gryskiewicz (Ed.) (1993, Stock #319) $30.00
Executive Selection: A Look at What We Know and What We Need to Know
D.L. DeVries (1993, Stock #321) $20.00
Healing the Wounds: Overcoming the Trauma of Layoffs and Revitalizing Downsized
Organizations D.M. Noer (1993, Stock #245) $27.50
If I'm In Charge Here, Why Is Everybody Laughing? D.P. Campbell (1984, Stock #205) $8.95
If You Don't Know Where You're Going You'll Probably End Up Somewhere Else
D.P. Campbell (1974, Stock #203) $9.40
Inklings: Collected Columns on Leadership and Creativity D.P. Campbell (1992, Stock #233) $15.00
Leadership Education 1996-1997: A Source Book (Sixth Edition), Vol. 1, Leadership Courses
and Programs F.H. Freeman, K.B. Knott, & M.K. Schwartz (Eds.) (1996, Stock #330) $35.00
Leadership Education 1996-1997: A Source Book (Sixth Edition), Vol. 2, Leadership Resources
F.H. Freeman, K.B. Knott, & M.K. Schwartz (Eds.) (1996, Stock #331) $35.00
Leadership: Enhancing the Lessons of Experience (Second Edition) R.L. Hughes, R.C. Ginnett,
& G.J. Curphy (1996, Stock #266) $49.95
The Lessons of Experience: How Successful Executives Develop on the Job M.W. McCall, Jr.,
M.M. Lombardo, & A.M. Morrison (1988, Stock #211) $22.95
Making Diversity Happen: Controversies and Solutions A.M. Morrison, M.N. Ruderman, &
M. Hughes-James (1993, Stock #320) $25.00
The New Leaders: Guidelines on Leadership Diversity in America A.M. Morrison
(1992, Stock #238) $29.00
Readings in Innovation S.S. Gryskiewicz & D.A. Hills (Eds.) (1992, Stock #240) $25.00
Selected Research on Work Team Diversity M.N. Ruderman, M.W. Hughes-James, &
S.E. Jackson (Eds.) (1996, Stock #326) $24.95
Take the Road to Creativity and Get Off Your Dead End D.P. Campbell (1977, Stock #204) $8.95
Whatever It Takes: The Realities of Managerial Decision Making (Second Edition)
M.W. McCall, Jr., & R.E. Kaplan (1990, Stock #218) $30.40
The Working Leader: The Triumph of High Performance Over Conventional Management
Principles L.R. Sayles (1993, Stock #243) $24.95

SPECIAL PACKAGES:

Conversations with CEOs (includes 310 & 316) $16.00
Development & Derailment (includes 136, 138, & 144) $25.00
The Diversity Collection (includes 145, 236, 238, 317, & 320) $85.00
Executive Selection Package (includes 141, 321, & 157) $32.00
Feedback to Managers—Volumes I & II (includes 149 & 150) $85.00
Personal Growth, Taking Charge, and Enhancing Creativity (includes 203, 204, & 205) $20.00
Leadership Education 1996-1997: A Source Book—Volumes 1 & 2 (includes 330 & 331) $60.00

Discounts are available. Please write for a comprehensive Publications catalog. Address your
request to: Publication, Center for Creative Leadership, P.O. Box 26300, Greensboro, NC 27438-
6300, 910-545-2805, or fax to 910-545-3221. All prices subject to change.

ORDER FORM

Name _____ Title _____

Organization _____

Mailing Address _____
(street address required for mailing)

City/State/Zip _____

Telephone _____ FAX _____
(telephone number required for UPS mailing)

Quantity	Stock No.	Title	Unit Cost	Amount

Subtotal	
Shipping and Handling (add 6% of subtotal with a $4.00 minimum; add 40% on all international shipping)	
NC residents add 6% sales tax; CA residents add 7.75% sales tax; CO residents add 6.2% sales tax	
TOTAL	

METHOD OF PAYMENT

❑ Check or money order enclosed (payable to Center for Creative Leadership).

❑ Purchase Order No. _____ (Must be accompanied by this form.)

❑ Charge my order, plus shipping, to my credit card:
   ❑ American Express   ❑ Discover   ❑ MasterCard   ❑ VISA

ACCOUNT NUMBER: _____ EXPIRATION DATE: MO.____ YR.____

NAME OF ISSUING BANK: _____

SIGNATURE _____

❑ Please put me on your mailing list.
❑ Please send me the Center's quarterly newsletter, *Issues & Observations.*

Publication • Center for Creative Leadership • P.O. Box 26300
Greensboro, NC 27438-6300
910-545-2805 • FAX 910-545-3221

Client Priority Code: R

fold here

_____

_____

_____

CENTER FOR CREATIVE LEADERSHIP
PUBLICATION
P.O. Box 26300
Greensboro, NC 27438-6300